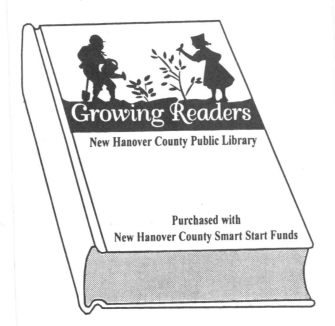

Kids in Their Communities™

I Live in a City

Stasia Ward Kehoe

The Rosen Publishing Group's
PowerKids Press™
New York

For Kevin, Thomas, and Mak

Published in 2000 by The Rosen Publishing Group, Inc.
29 East 21st Street, New York, NY 10010

First Edition

Book Design: Michael de Guzman

Photo Credits and Photo Illustrations: pp. 4, 7, 8, 11, 12, 15 by Brent Jones; p. 16 CORBIS/Sandy Felsenthal; p. 19 CORBIS/MAGELLAN Geographix; p. 20 CORBIS/Charles E. Rotkin.

Kehoe, Stasia Ward.
  I live in a city / by Stasia Ward Kehoe.
          p.   cm. – (Kids in their communities)
  Includes index.
Summary: Eight-year-old Jasmin, who lives in Chicago, describes her school, favorite sites to visit, and her city's government, arts, sports, neighborhoods, and tall buildings.
  ISBN 0-8239-5437-4
1. Chicago (Ill.) – Social life and customs – Juvenile literature. 2. City and town life – Illinois – Chicago Juvenile literature. 3. Children – Illinois – Chicago – Social life and customs Juvenile literature.
[1. Chicago (Ill.) 2. City and town life. 3. Cities and towns.] I. Title. II. Series: Kehoe, Stasia Ward, 1968–   Kids in their communities.
F548.52.K45 1999
977.3'11 – dc21   99-25628
                                                       CIP

Manufactured in the United States of America

CONTENTS

Jasmin

My name is Jasmin. I am eight years old. I live with my mother, father, brother, and sister in the city of Chicago. Cities are full of big buildings, rushing traffic, and lots of people. Chicago is a beautiful city because it sits right next to Lake Michigan and has lots of beaches and parks.

◀ *Chicago is called the "Windy City" because we get lots of windy weather.*

Ukrainian Village

My neighborhood is called Ukrainian Village. Many Polish, Italian, and Hispanic Americans live in Ukrainian Village. It is a nice place to live because there are lots of bakeries, restaurants, and beautiful churches. Chicago has 77 different and interesting neighborhoods, such as Chinatown, Garfield Park, Greektown, Lincoln Park, Pilsen, River North, and Woodlawn.

There are many churches in my neighborhood. I love to hear their bells ring.

Skyscrapers

Chicago is a city with tall and beautiful buildings. My parents told me that famous architects have lived and worked here. The world's first skyscraper was designed in Chicago in 1885. It was called the Home Insurance Building. The architect's name was William Le Baron Jenney. The Sears Tower is another famous skyscraper in Chicago. It is 1,454 feet high, which makes it one of the tallest buildings in the world.

◄ *Very tall buildings like the Sears Tower are called skyscrapers because it looks like their roofs are touching the sky.*

Out and About

If you want to travel around Chicago, you can ride in a car, a taxi, or a bus. You can also ride the **elevated** trains. In the city, we call the elevated train the "EL" for short. The "EL" travels on tracks that are raised high above the ground. Chicago was the first city to have an elevated railway. It began running in 1892. To ride the "EL," you go to a train station and buy a token. You have to drop your token into a slot to get through the **turnstile**. Then you wait for the train.

You need a token or a special card called a transit card to ride the train.

School

My school is not a public school. It is a **parochial** school run by the **Catholic Archdiocese** of Chicago. One thing that makes my school different than public school is that we have religion class. Another thing is that all the students at my school have to wear **uniforms**. Our uniforms are red, white, blue, and beige. Sometimes I wish I could choose something more exciting to wear!

◀ Every day that I go to school, I have to wear a uniform.

City Arts

In Chicago, there are lots of ways to enjoy arts and **culture**. The Art Institute of Chicago is one of many museums you can visit. There are over 150 theaters and performing groups like the Second City **Comedy Troupe**. Chicago also has over 6,000 restaurants. You can taste great food every year at The Taste of Chicago, the biggest outdoor food festival in the United States!

Another neat place you can visit in Chicago is the Adler Planetarium. ▶

City Sports

Sports are another big part of city life. Chicago's two baseball teams are called the Cubs and the White Sox. The Blackhawks are our hockey team. Our football team is called the Bears. Michael Jordan used to play basketball for the Chicago Bulls. He helped the Bulls win six national titles. Even though he doesn't play basketball anymore, Michael Jordan is still one of Chicago's superstars.

 Michael Jordan played many games with the Bulls at United Center.

Chicago Government

I learned about Chicago's history and government in my social studies class. My teacher told us that Chicago became a city in 1837. Back then, only about 4,000 people lived here. Today, almost three million people live in Chicago. We also learned that Chicago is divided into 50 wards. Each ward has its own alderman or alderwoman. These people belong to the Chicago City Council, which works with the mayor to keep the city running smoothly.

Chicago is divided into smaller sections, called wards, to help the government get jobs done.

Big Chicago

How big is the city of Chicago? Here are some facts I've learned about my favorite city! Chicago has the world's largest public library. It holds over two million books. The world's largest cookie factory is in Chicago. Nabisco made over 4.6 billion Oreo cookies at the factory in 1996. Chicago has the world's busiest airport. Each day, more people get on planes at Chicago's O'Hare International Airport than at any other airport in the world.

If you travel to another country, you might fly through O'Hare International Airport.

City Life

   Like other cities, Chicago has its problems. There are so many cars that sometimes traffic gets backed up and it takes a long time to get around. The city also has to worry about air and water **pollution**. Even though people in Chicago have to deal with the problems of having lots of people, cars, and buildings so close together, I still love it here. It is a great place to live because there are always neat places to go and fun things to do.

Glossary

Archdiocese (arch-DY-uh-sis) An area or territory run by a religious leader called an archbishop.

architects (AR-kuh-teks) People who design buildings.

Catholic (KATH-lik) Someone who belongs to the Catholic religion, which is part of the Christian faith.

comedy (KAH-mih-dee) Something meant to be funny or make people laugh.

culture (KUL-chur) Social and artistic activities.

elevated (EH-luh-vay-tid) To be raised above the ground.

parochial (puh-ROH-kee-ul) Relating to a church community.

pollution (puh-LOO-shin) Man-made waste that harms the environment.

skyscraper (SKY-skray-pur) A very tall building.

troupe (TROOP) A group of theater performers.

turnstile (TERN-styl) A stand with spinning arms that only one person can pass through at a time.

uniforms (YOO-nih-fohrmz) Special clothes worn at school or a job.

Index

Web Site:
http://www.ci.chi.il.us./Tourism/
Downtown/

24